U.S.A. TRAVEL GUIDES

MISSOURI

BY ANN HEINRICHS • ILLUSTRATED BY MATT KANIA

The Child's World®
childsworld.com

Published by The Child's World®
1980 Lookout Drive • Mankato, MN 56003-1705
800-599-READ • www.childsworld.com

ISBN 9781503819658
LCCN 2016961178

Printing
Printed in the United States of America
PA02334

Ann Heinrichs is the author of more than 100 books for children and young adults. She has also enjoyed successful careers as a children's book editor and an advertising copywriter. Ann grew up in Fort Smith, Arkansas, and lives in Chicago, Illinois.

About the Author
Ann Heinrichs

Matt Kania loves maps and, as a kid, dreamed of making them. In school he studied geography and cartography, and today he makes maps for a living. Matt's favorite thing about drawing maps is learning about the places they represent. Many of the maps he has created can be found in books, magazines, videos, Web sites, and public places.

About the
Map Illustrator
Matt Kania

*On the cover: The St. Louis Arch towers
over downtown St. Louis.*

OUR MISSOURI TRIP

Missouri 4

Meramec Caverns near Stanton 7

Fun at Lake of the Ozarks 8

Branson's Silver Dollar City 11

The White Squirrels of Marionville 12

Historic Ste. Geneviève 15

Missouri Town 1855 16

Saint Louis and the Gateway Arch 19

German Festivals in Hermann 20

Athens Battlefield and the U.S. Civil War 23

Bollinger Mill near Burfordville 24

Marshall's Corn Husking Championship 27

The State Capitol in Jefferson City 28

Boeing's Air and Space Exhibit 31

Pet Tricks at Purina Farms 32

Tom Sawyer Days in Hannibal 35

Our Trip 36
State Flag and Seal 37
State Symbols 37
State Song 37
Famous People 38
Words to Know 38
To Learn More 39
Index 40

MISSOURI

Ready for a tour of the Show-Me State? That's Missouri! You'll find lots to see and do there. Just say, "Show me!"

You'll meet Mark Twain and Harry Truman. You'll wander through spooky caves. You'll see white squirrels and take wild rides. And you'll watch dogs doing cool tricks. Just follow that loopy dotted line. Or else skip around. Either way, you're in for a great adventure. So buckle up and settle in. We're on our way!

WELCOME TO MISSOURI

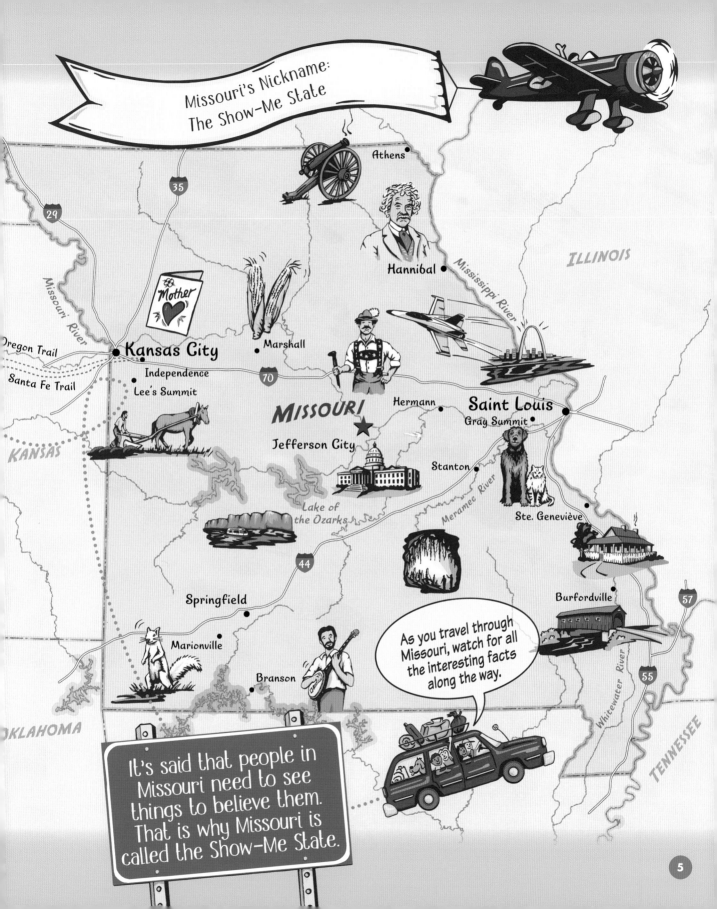

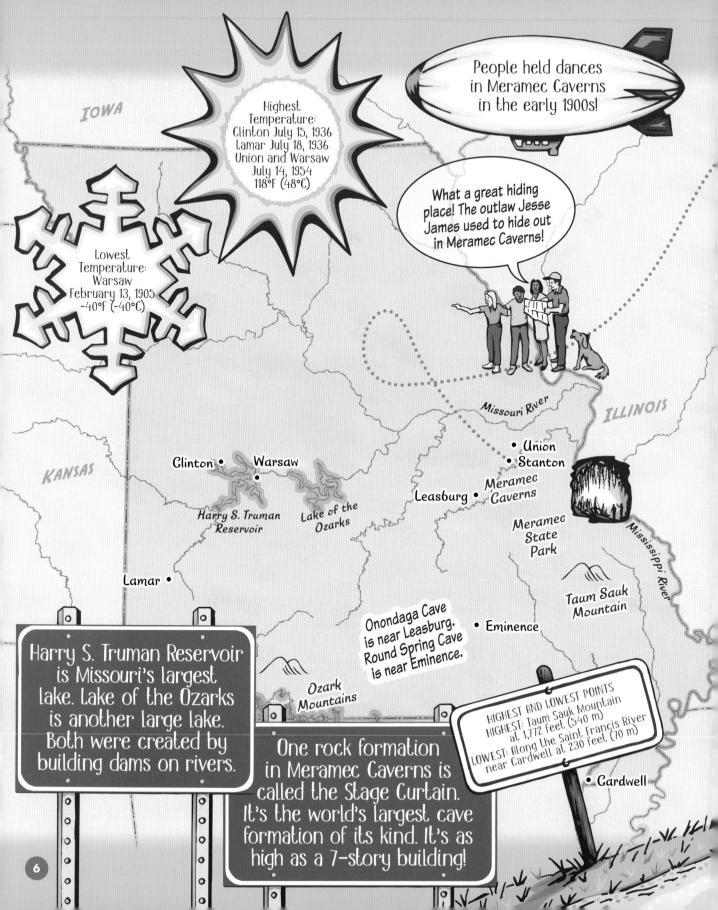

IOWA

Highest
Temperature:
Clinton July 15, 1936
Lamar July 18, 1936
Union and Warsaw
July 14, 1954
118°F (48°C)

People held dances
in Meramec Caverns
in the early 1900s!

Lowest
Temperature:
Warsaw
February 13, 1905
-40°F (-40°C)

What a great hiding
place! The outlaw Jesse
James used to hide out
in Meramec Caverns!

Missouri River

ILLINOIS

KANSAS

Clinton •   • Warsaw

• Union
• Stanton

Leasburg •   Meramec
            Caverns

Harry S. Truman
Reservoir

Lake of the
Ozarks

Meramec
State
Park

Mississippi River

Lamar •

Taum Sauk
Mountain

Onondaga Cave
is near Leasburg.
Round Spring Cave
is near Eminence.

• Eminence

Harry S. Truman Reservoir
is Missouri's largest
lake. Lake of the Ozarks
is another large lake.
Both were created by
building dams on rivers.

Ozark
Mountains

HIGHEST AND LOWEST POINTS
HIGHEST: Taum Sauk Mountain
    at 1,772 feet (540 m)
LOWEST: Along the Saint Francis River
    near Cardwell at 230 feet (70 m)

One rock formation
in Meramec Caverns is
called the Stage Curtain.
It's the world's largest cave
formation of its kind. It's as
high as a 7-story building!

• Cardwell

You're deep inside the cave. Awesome rock formations are everywhere. Some hang down from high overhead. Others reach up from the floor. They sparkle like jewels!

You're exploring Meramec Caverns near Stanton. It's just one of Missouri's thousands of caves. They were carved by underground rivers. Missouri has lots of natural water springs, too.

The Ozark Mountains rise in southern Missouri. Many streams wind through their forested hills. Rolling plains cover northern Missouri. This is a rich farming region. The Mississippi River forms Missouri's eastern border. The Missouri River flows across the whole state. It's the Mississippi River's longest **tributary**.

The Meramec Caverns are located at Meramec State Park.

FUN AT LAKE OF THE OZARKS

Zoom around the lake in a boat. Speed along on water skis. Go swimming or fishing. Or just be lazy and sunbathe. You're enjoying Lake of the Ozarks! This huge lake is a popular vacation spot. Some people enjoy the Ozarks' forests and streams. They like hiking, camping, and watching wildlife.

Missouri has many museums and historic sites. Its sports teams draw big crowds, too. Whatever you enjoy, you'll find it in Missouri!

Lake of the Ozarks is so large that its total shoreline is longer than the coastline of California!

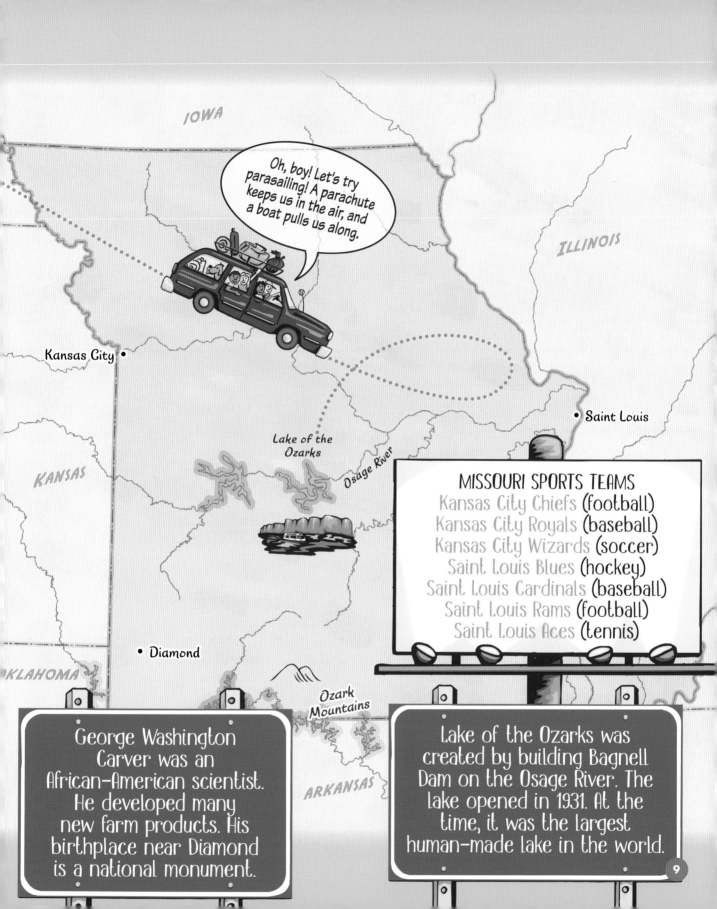

Oh, boy! Let's try parasailing! A parachute keeps us in the air, and a boat pulls us along.

IOWA

ILLINOIS

Kansas City •

• Saint Louis

Lake of the Ozarks

Osage River

KANSAS

MISSOURI SPORTS TEAMS
Kansas City Chiefs (football)
Kansas City Royals (baseball)
Kansas City Wizards (soccer)
Saint Louis Blues (hockey)
Saint Louis Cardinals (baseball)
Saint Louis Rams (football)
Saint Louis Aces (tennis)

• Diamond

OKLAHOMA

Ozark Mountains

George Washington Carver was an African-American scientist. He developed many new farm products. His birthplace near Diamond is a national monument.

Lake of the Ozarks was created by building Bagnell Dam on the Osage River. The lake opened in 1931. At the time, it was the largest human-made lake in the world.

ARKANSAS

9

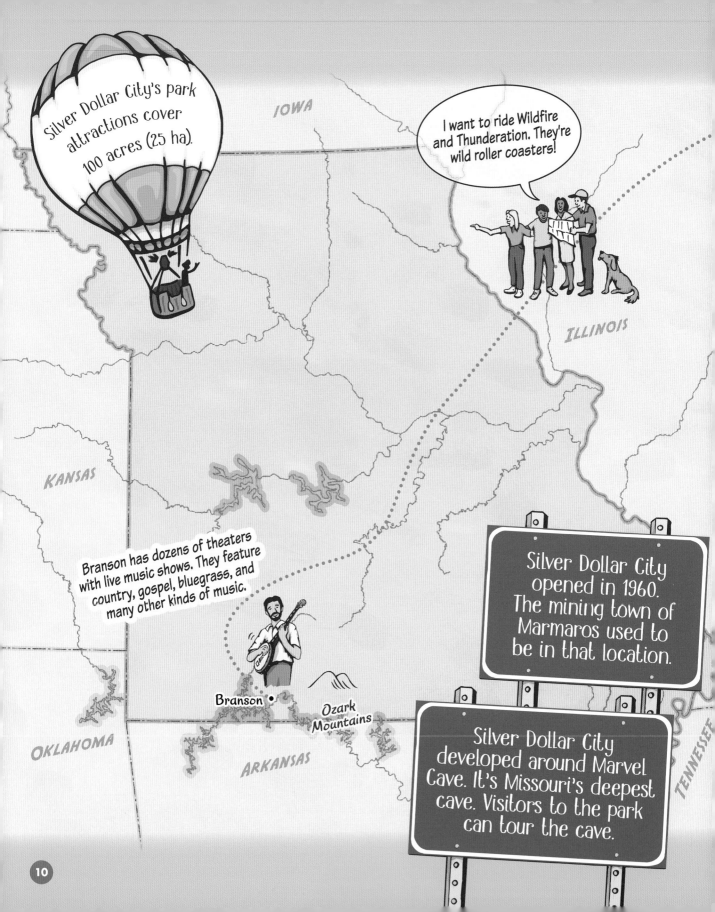

Silver Dollar City's park attractions cover 100 acres (25 ha).

I want to ride Wildfire and Thunderation. They're wild roller coasters!

IOWA

ILLINOIS

KANSAS

Branson has dozens of theaters with live music shows. They feature country, gospel, bluegrass, and many other kinds of music.

Branson

Ozark Mountains

OKLAHOMA

ARKANSAS

TENNESSEE

Silver Dollar City opened in 1960. The mining town of Marmaros used to be in that location.

Silver Dollar City developed around Marvel Cave. It's Missouri's deepest cave. Visitors to the park can tour the cave.

BRANSON'S SILVER DOLLAR CITY

You could spend days at Silver Dollar City! It's built like an old Ozarks mining town. Stroll around the theme park. You'll see people working on **pioneer** crafts. Some are blowing glass or making pottery. Some are making candy or candles. You'll see blacksmiths and wood-carvers, too.

Maybe you'd like the rides. Try the American Plunge. You drop down five stories and get splashed. Do you really want to get wet? Then twist and turn on the Lost River of the Ozarks. Or ride the Frisco Dollar Line Steam Train. Watch out, though. Some crazy train robbers will jump on!

Silver Dollar City has plenty of attractions to keep everyone entertained.

THE WHITE SQUIRRELS OF MARIONVILLE

Something white and furry scurries across the park. What can it be? If you're in Marionville, it's a white squirrel!

Marionville is famous for its white squirrels. They eat corn, nuts, and sunflower seeds. Try being really quiet and still. They may take food from your hand! Most of Missouri's squirrels are gray. They live wherever there are lots of trees. Forests in the Ozarks are home to many animals. Deer are the biggest of them. Smaller animals include skunks, beavers, foxes, and rabbits. Quail live mostly on the ground. These birds are sometimes called bobwhites. That's because their call sounds like "bob-white!"

No one knows for sure how the white squirrels first came to Marionville.

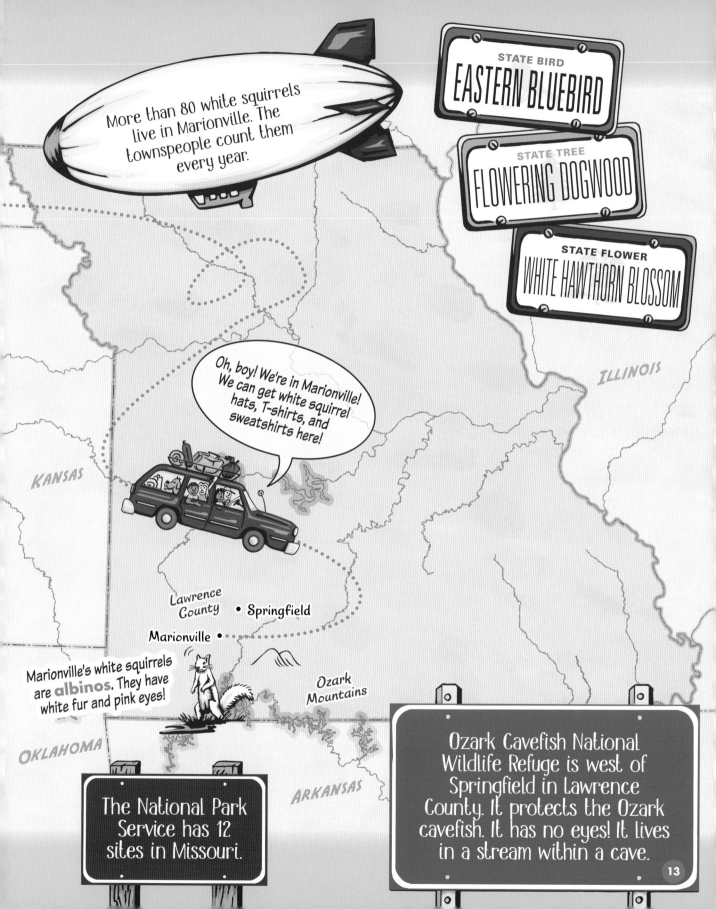

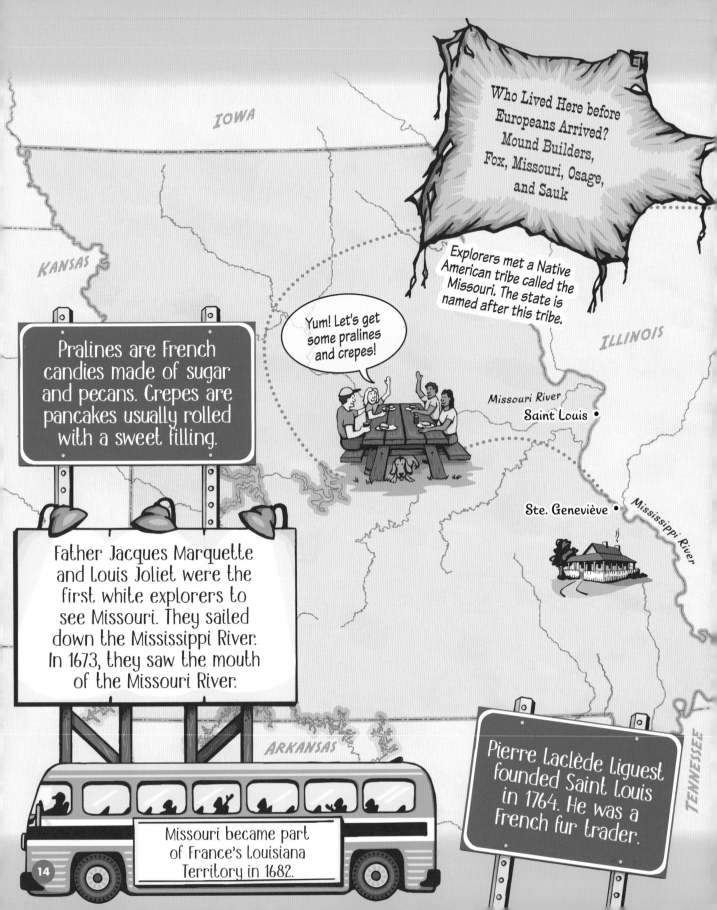

Who Lived Here before Europeans Arrived? Mound Builders, Fox, Missouri, Osage, and Sauk

IOWA

KANSAS

Explorers met a Native American tribe called the Missouri. The state is named after this tribe.

ILLINOIS

Yum! Let's get some pralines and crepes!

Pralines are French candies made of sugar and pecans. Crepes are pancakes usually rolled with a sweet filling.

Missouri River

Saint Louis •

Ste. Geneviève •

Mississippi River

Father Jacques Marquette and Louis Joliet were the first white explorers to see Missouri. They sailed down the Mississippi River. In 1673, they saw the mouth of the Missouri River.

ARKANSAS

TENNESSEE

Pierre Laclède Liguest founded Saint Louis in 1764. He was a French fur trader.

Missouri became part of France's Louisiana Territory in 1682.

14

HISTORIC STE. GENEVIÈVE

Stop by Ste. Geneviève's French Festival. It celebrates the city's **heritage**. You'll see folk dancers kicking up their heels. French folk songs fill the air. Townspeople act out historic events. And they're all dressed in old French costumes.

Ste., or Saint, Geneviève is Missouri's oldest city. French people founded it in 1735.

French explorers were the first Europeans in Missouri. Those explorers originally went to Canada. Then they sailed down the Mississippi River to Missouri. There they met many Native Americans such as the Illinois, Missouri, and Osage. French fur traders set up trading posts. They traded with the Native Americans for furs. French **missionaries** came, too. They taught Christianity to the Native Americans.

The town of Ste. Geneviève was named after the patron, or protecting, saint of Paris.

The United States gained Missouri in 1803. No one knew much about lands farther west. Meriwether Lewis and William Clark explored those lands. They set out from Saint Louis in 1804.

Soon settlers began farming in Missouri. Want to see how they lived? Just visit Missouri Town 1855. It's near Lee's Summit. People there are dressed in 1800s outfits. They're doing farm chores and other daily activities. They explain their work. And you can pet the farm animals!

Thousands of pioneers headed west from Missouri. They took the Santa Fe and Oregon trails. Both of these trails began in Independence.

In the 1800s, many people chopped their own wood and lived in log cabins.

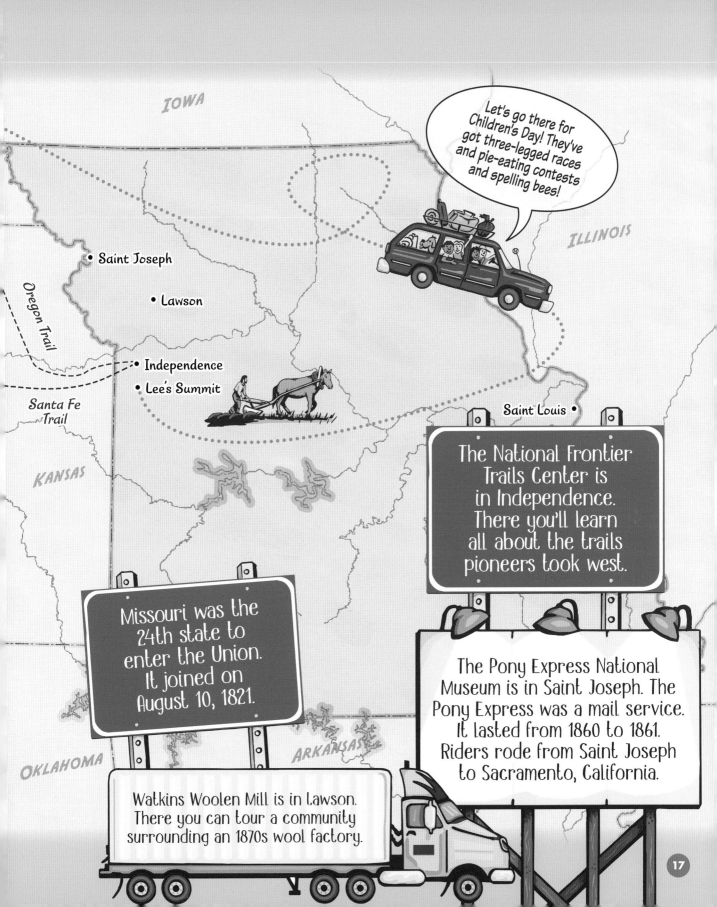

Let's go there for Children's Day! They've got three-legged races and pie-eating contests and spelling bees!

IOWA

ILLINOIS

Saint Joseph

Lawson

Oregon Trail

Independence

Lee's Summit

Santa Fe Trail

Saint Louis

KANSAS

The National Frontier Trails Center is in Independence. There you'll learn all about the trails pioneers took west.

Missouri was the 24th state to enter the Union. It joined on August 10, 1821.

The Pony Express National Museum is in Saint Joseph. The Pony Express was a mail service. It lasted from 1860 to 1861. Riders rode from Saint Joseph to Sacramento, California.

OKLAHOMA

ARKANSAS

Watkins Woolen Mill is in Lawson. There you can tour a community surrounding an 1870s wool factory.

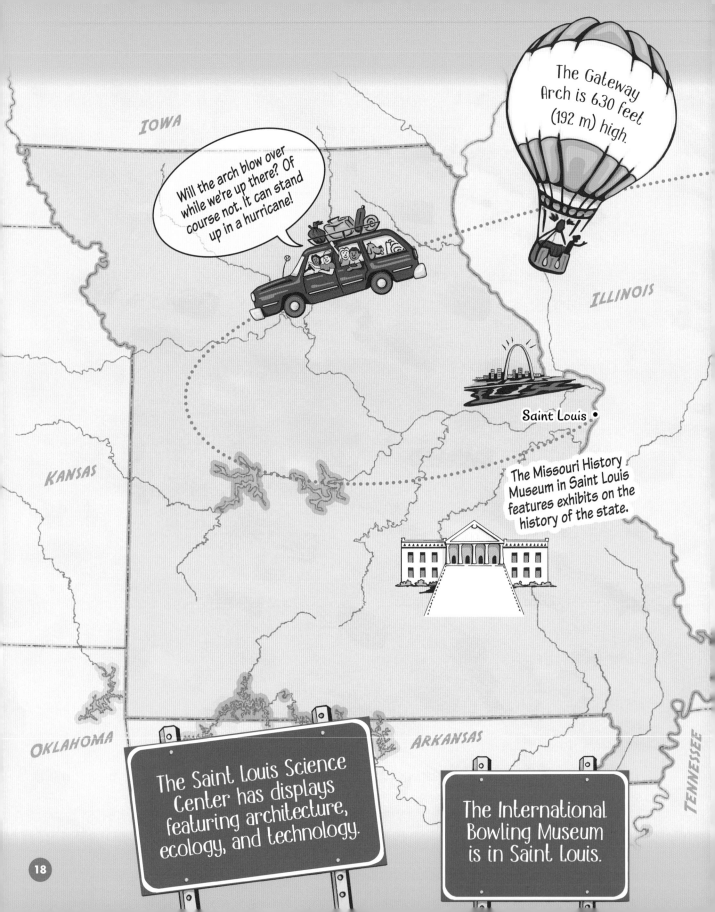

Ride to the top of the Gateway **Arch**. It's taller than two Statues of Liberty! Look around, and you'll see awesome views. Does it feel like the arch is moving? Don't worry. It's built to sway in the wind!

Saint Louis is called the Gateway to the West. Many pioneers began traveling west from there. That's how the Gateway Arch got its name.

Saint Louis has many fun places to visit. You'll see animal shows at the city's zoo. Then explore the Saint Louis Science Center. You can try digging for dinosaur bones there! The city has many other museums and parks. Take time to see them all!

The Gateway Arch is as wide as it is tall.

GERMAN FESTIVALS IN HERMANN

Do you like sausage? Then Hermann is the place for you! This town has lots of German festivals. And they all serve plenty of sausage!

Wurstfest takes place in March. You can watch experts make sausage there. And you can fill your tummy with sausage! May is the time for Maifest. Children dress up and march in a parade. And people sell sausages. Octoberfest is in October, of course. There you'll eat German cakes and sauerkraut. And more sausage!

Germans were among Missouri's early settlers. Many other people moved to Missouri. They came from Europe, Asia, and Spanish-speaking lands.

Bratwurst and sauerkraut, or fermented cabbage, are popular German dishes.

Yum! Which do I want? Knackwurst or bratwurst?

Deutschheim State Historic Site is a German **culture** center in Hermann.

IOWA

ILLINOIS

KANSAS

• Kansas City

In 2016, 6,093,000 people lived in Missouri. It's the 18th-largest state by population.

Hermann • • Berger

Saint Louis

Augusta

Westphalia •

Koeltztown •

Ste. Geneviève celebrates French culture with the Bastille Days and Jour de Fête festivals.

Ste. Geneviève •

Altenburg

Springfield •

POPULATION OF LARGEST CITIES
Kansas City.................475,378
Saint Louis..................315,685
Springfield..................166,810

OKLAHOMA

TENNESSEE

German people settled many Missouri towns. Some of those towns are Hermann, Altenburg, Westphalia, Augusta, Koeltztown, and Berger.

Kansas City holds a huge Saint Patrick's Day parade. Saint Patrick is the patron saint of Ireland. His feast day is March 17.

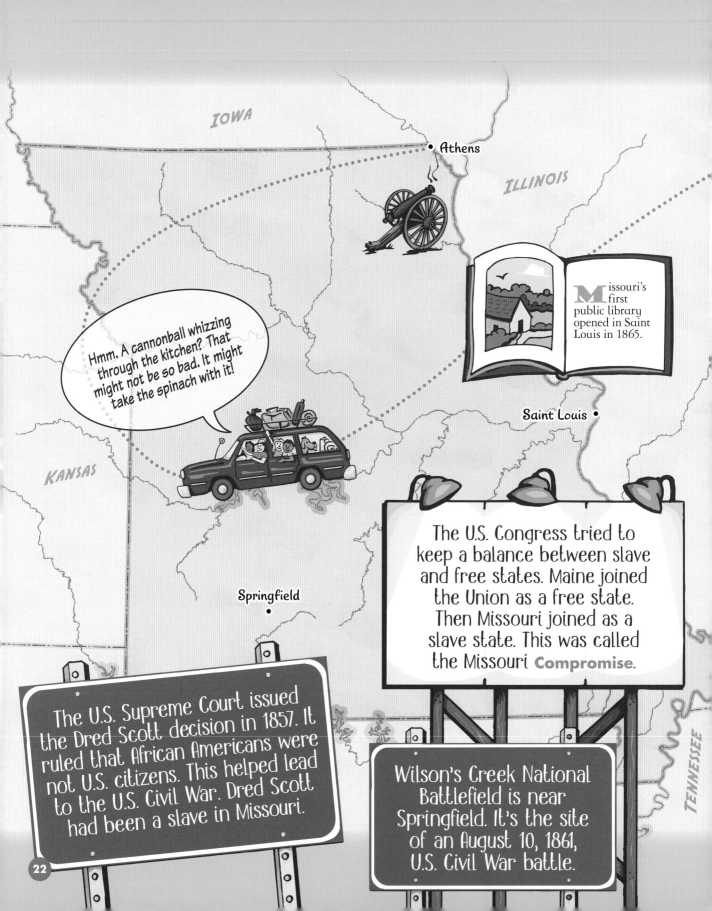

IOWA

• Athens

ILLINOIS

Missouri's first public library opened in Saint Louis in 1865.

Hmm. A cannonball whizzing through the kitchen? That might not be so bad. It might take the spinach with it!

Saint Louis •

KANSAS

Springfield
•

The U.S. Congress tried to keep a balance between slave and free states. Maine joined the Union as a free state. Then Missouri joined as a slave state. This was called the Missouri **Compromise**.

The U.S. Supreme Court issued the Dred Scott decision in 1857. It ruled that African Americans were not U.S. citizens. This helped lead to the U.S. Civil War. Dred Scott had been a slave in Missouri.

Wilson's Creek National Battlefield is near Springfield. It's the site of an August 10, 1861, U.S. Civil War battle.

TENNESSEE

ATHENS BATTLEFIELD AND THE U.S. CIVIL WAR

Imagine a **cannonball** smashing through your kitchen wall. That's what happened to a house in Athens. A cannonball shot two holes through the kitchen! You can see them, too. Just visit the Battle of Athens State Historic Site.

This battle took place during the U.S. Civil War (1861–1865). Northern and Southern states were fighting over slavery. Northerners were against using African Americans as slaves. But Southern states wanted to keep slavery.

People on both sides lived in Missouri. It was a state that allowed slavery. But Missouri joined the North in the war. After the North won, the slaves were freed. However, there was a long struggle for equality of all races.

Many U.S. Civil War battles are reenacted throughout Missouri.

BOLLINGER MILL NEAR BURFORDVILLE

Do you know what a mill is? It's an early type of factory. Mills were built beside rivers. The water turned the mill's big wheel around. The turning wheel powered the mill's machines.

Want to see a working mill? Just visit Bollinger Mill near Burfordville. It ground wheat into flour. It also ground corn into cornmeal. And it's still grinding away!

Soybeans and corn are important Missouri products. So are cattle and hogs. People shipped their products to big-city markets. Saint Louis and Kansas City became trade centers. They were transportation centers, too. Goods came through on railroads and steamboats.

Cross the covered bridge and tour Bollinger Mill!

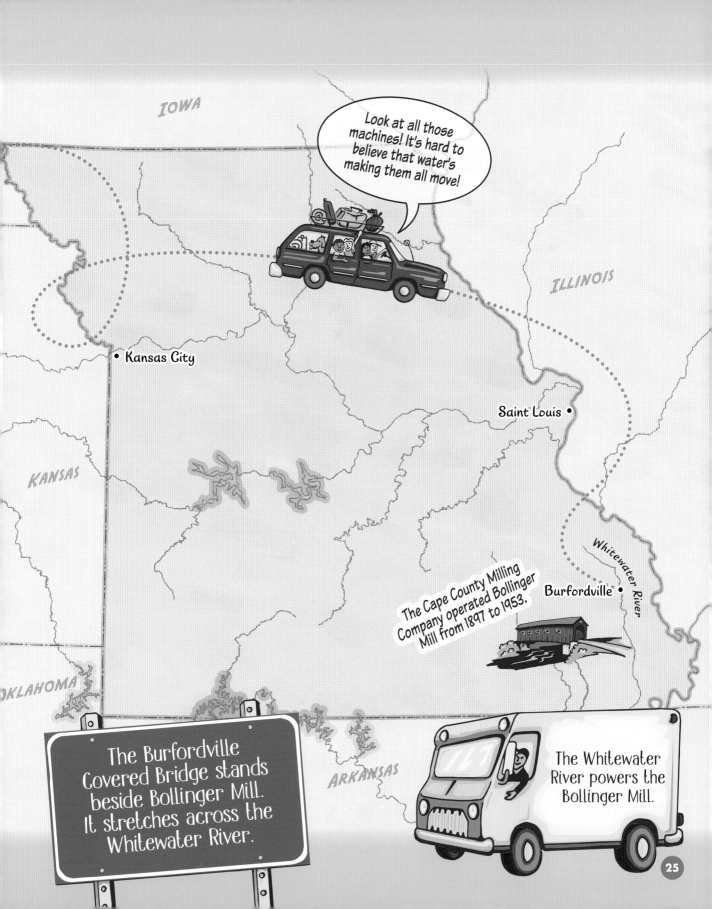

Look at all those machines! It's hard to believe that water's making them all move!

IOWA

ILLINOIS

• Kansas City

Saint Louis •

KANSAS

Whitewater River

The Cape County Milling Company operated Bollinger Mill from 1897 to 1953.

Burfordville •

OKLAHOMA

ARKANSAS

The Burfordville Covered Bridge stands beside Bollinger Mill. It stretches across the Whitewater River.

The Whitewater River powers the Bollinger Mill.

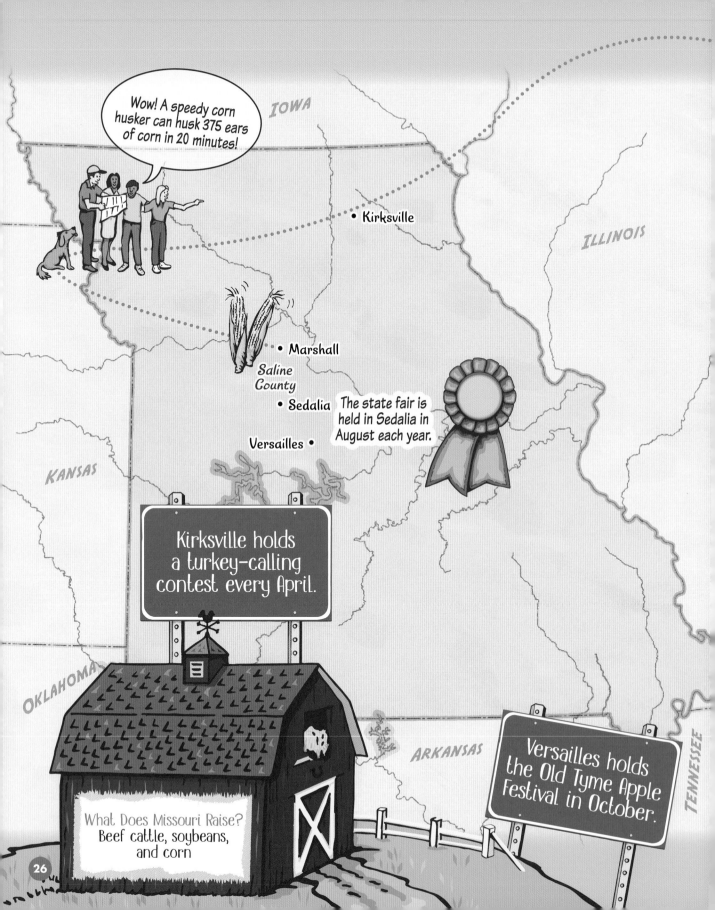

MARSHALL'S CORN HUSKING CHAMPIONSHIP

Are you a good corn husker? Then try the Missouri State Corn Husking Championship in Marshall. Husking means ripping off the husk. That's the leafy covering on an ear of corn. Can you keep up?

This contest is part of the Saline County Fair. Besides husking, there's plenty to do there. You can hunt for money in a corn pile. Or you can enter the corn-throwing contest. Do you like animals? Find your favorite animal at the petting zoo.

Missourians love to celebrate their farm **traditions**. Beef cattle and hogs are the top farm products. Chickens and dairy cattle are important, too. Soybeans are the top crop. But corn's a lot more fun!

The Corn Husking Championship has several age groups in which to compete.

Take a tour of the state capitol. You'll get a real education. And you don't have to read a thing! There's a big room on the first floor. Step inside, and your jaw will drop. All the walls are brightly painted. They show scenes from Missouri's history.

Inside the capitol are important state government offices. Missouri's government has three branches. The General Assembly forms one branch. Its members make the state laws. The governor heads another branch. It carries out the laws. Judges make up the third branch. They decide whether laws have been broken.

The dome inside the capitol is 238 feet (73 m) tall!

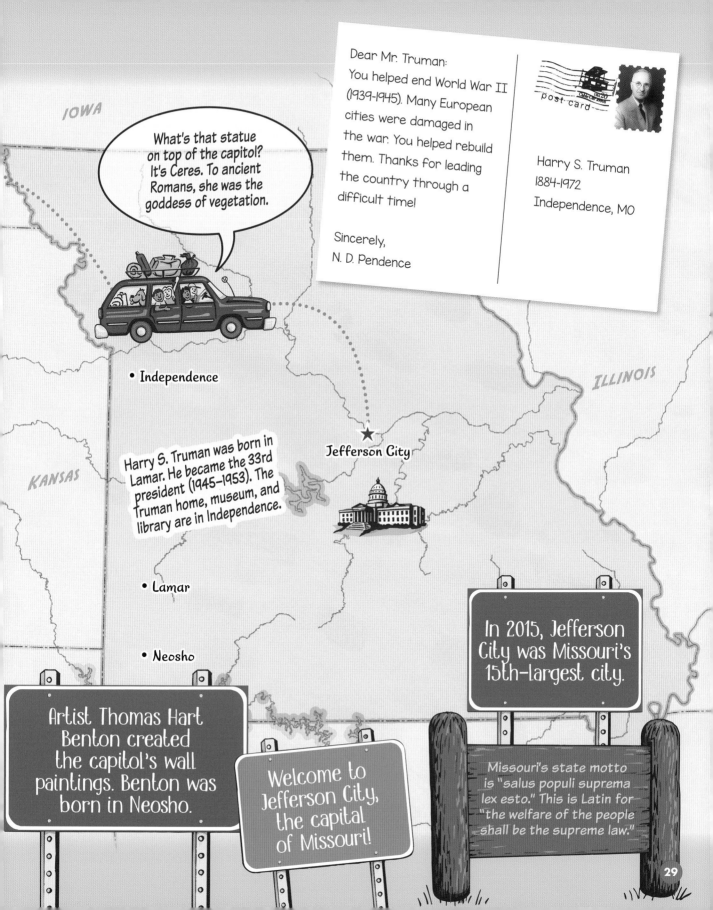

What's that statue on top of the capitol? It's Ceres. To ancient Romans, she was the goddess of vegetation.

Dear Mr. Truman:
You helped end World War II (1939-1945). Many European cities were damaged in the war. You helped rebuild them. Thanks for leading the country through a difficult time!

Sincerely,
N. D. Pendence

post card

Harry S. Truman
1884-1972
Independence, MO

• Independence

Harry S. Truman was born in Lamar. He became the 33rd president (1945–1953). The Truman home, museum, and library are in Independence.

★ Jefferson City

• Lamar

• Neosho

In 2015, Jefferson City was Missouri's 15th-largest city.

Artist Thomas Hart Benton created the capitol's wall paintings. Benton was born in Neosho.

Welcome to Jefferson City, the capital of Missouri!

Missouri's state motto is "salus populi suprema lex esto." This is Latin for "the welfare of the people shall be the supreme law."

IOWA

ILLINOIS

KANSAS

29

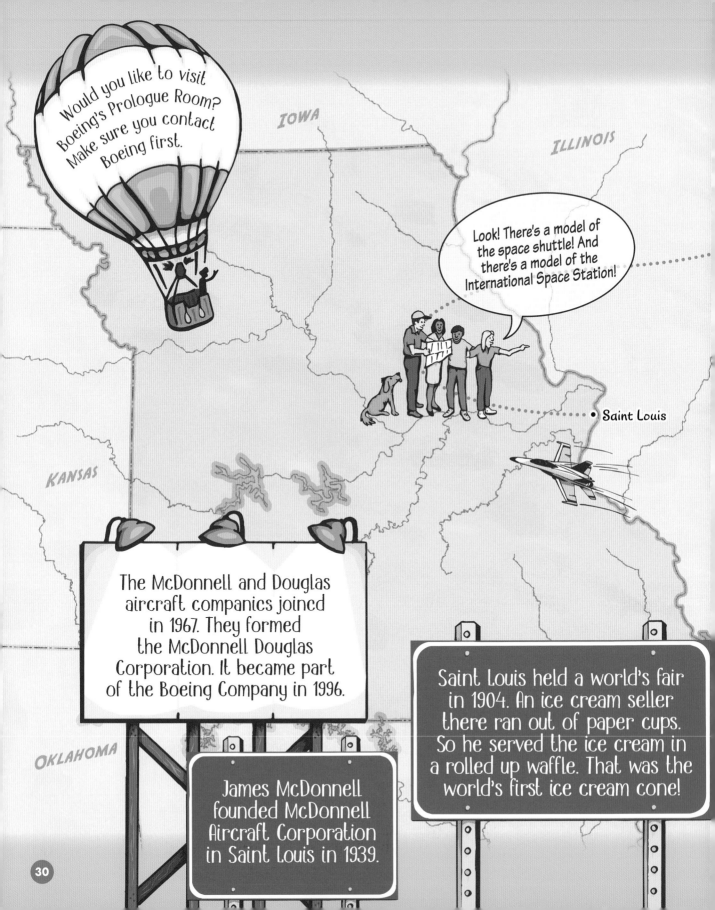

BOEING'S AIR AND SPACE EXHIBIT

Do you like airplanes and spacecraft? Then check out the Air and Space Exhibit. It's at the Boeing Company's James S. McDonnell Prologue Room in Saint Louis. You'll see giant airplane models. You'll also see life-size models of space capsules. They're a lot like a very famous spacecraft. Why are they famous? They carried the first U.S. astronauts into space!

Farming was once Missouri's major **industry**. But new industries took over in the mid-1900s. New factories made electronics, airplanes, and other goods.

McDonnell Douglas became a huge Saint Louis company. It made aircraft for the U.S. armed forces. It also made airplanes for regular travel. Now McDonnell Douglas is part of Boeing.

The model airplanes on display at the Prologue Room are based on real airplanes!

PET TRICKS AT PURINA FARMS

The dog sits up tall. It jumps up and then rolls over. Good doggie! You're visiting Purina Farms in Gray Summit. And you're watching a dog **obedience** show!

Purina Farms is a pet food factory. It's great fun to visit. You'll cuddle with puppies and kittens. You'll milk cows and play in the hay. And you'll learn about caring for your pet.

Missouri factories make much more than pet food. The top factory products are things that go! That means aircraft, train cars, trucks, and cars. Foods are also important factory products. These include milk, meats, flour, and beer. Yes, and pet food, too!

Many breeds of dogs compete in the Purina Dog Show.

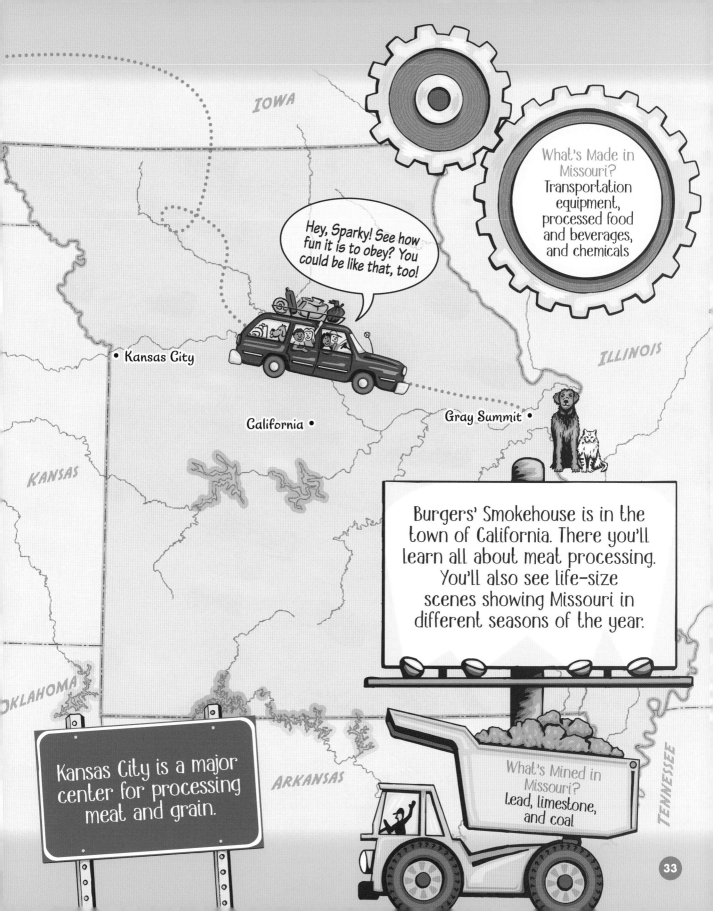

IOWA

What's Made in Missouri? Transportation equipment, processed food and beverages, and chemicals

Hey, Sparky! See how fun it is to obey? You could be like that, too!

ILLINOIS

• Kansas City

California •

Gray Summit •

Burgers' Smokehouse is in the town of California. There you'll learn all about meat processing. You'll also see life-size scenes showing Missouri in different seasons of the year.

KANSAS

OKLAHOMA

Kansas City is a major center for processing meat and grain.

ARKANSAS

What's Mined in Missouri? Lead, limestone, and coal

TENNESSEE

33

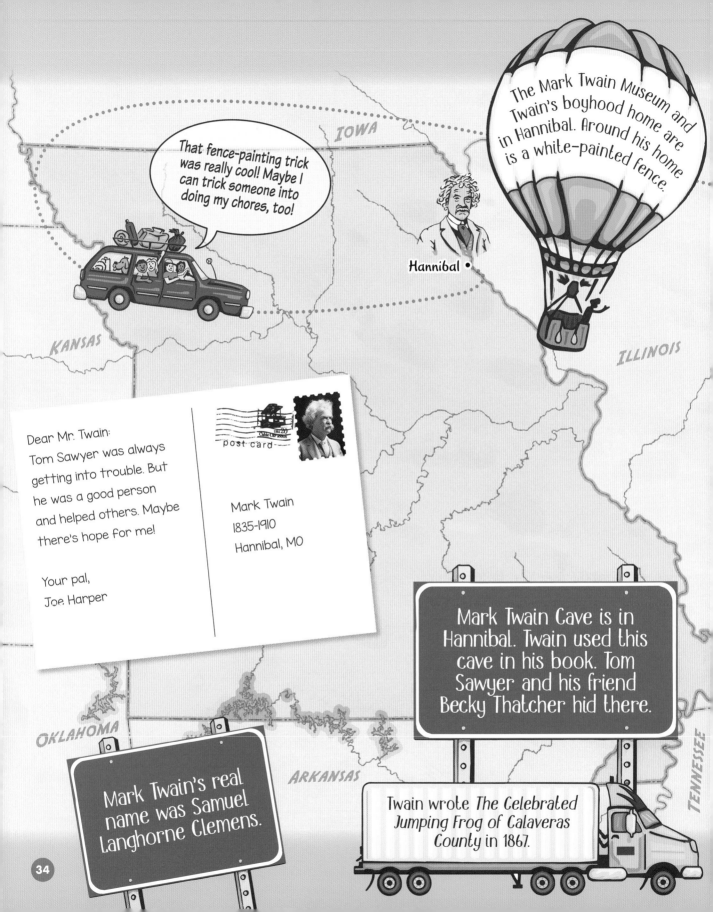

That fence-painting trick was really cool! Maybe I can trick someone into doing my chores, too!

IOWA

The Mark Twain Museum and Twain's boyhood home are in Hannibal. Around his home is a white-painted fence.

Hannibal •

KANSAS

ILLINOIS

Dear Mr. Twain:
Tom Sawyer was always getting into trouble. But he was a good person and helped others. Maybe there's hope for me!

Your pal,
Joe Harper

post card

Mark Twain
1835-1910
Hannibal, MO

OKLAHOMA

ARKANSAS

TENNESSEE

Mark Twain's real name was Samuel Langhorne Clemens.

Mark Twain Cave is in Hannibal. Twain used this cave in his book. Tom Sawyer and his friend Becky Thatcher hid there.

Twain wrote *The Celebrated Jumping Frog of Calaveras County* in 1867.

Are you good at painting? Try the fence-painting contest. Do you have a frog? It can enter the jumping frog contest. These are some events during Tom Sawyer Days!

Tom Sawyer was a boy in a famous book. It's called *The Adventures of Tom Sawyer*. Mark Twain, the author, grew up in Hannibal. The town celebrates Twain with Tom Sawyer Days. Twain used real people in his books. He just changed their names. Tom may be based on Twain himself. One day, Tom had to paint a fence. He told his friends that fence painting is fun. So they finished the job for him!

Visit Mark Twain's childhood home during Tom Sawyer Days.

OUR TRIP

We visited many amazing places on our trip! We also met a lot of interesting people along the way. Look at the map below. Use your finger to trace all the places we have been.

What famous outlaw hid in Meramec Caverns? *See page 6 for the answer.*

What year was the Lake of the Ozarks created? *Page 9 has the answer.*

What is Missouri's deepest cave? *See page 10 for the answer.*

Where is the International Bowling Museum? *Look on page 18 for the answer.*

Where is the state fair held each year? *Page 26 has the answer.*

What is the capital of Missouri? *Turn to page 29 for the answer.*

What was invented at the 1904 World's Fair? *Look on page 30 for the answer.*

What was Mark Twain's real name? *Turn to page 34 for the answer.*

Athens

Hannibal

Mississippi River

Missouri River

Oregon Trail

Santa Fe Trail

Kansas City

Independence

Lee's Summit

Marshall

MISSOURI

Jefferson City

Lake of the Ozarks

Hermann

ILLINOIS

Saint Louis

Gray Summit

Stanton

Meramec River

Ste. Geneviève

KANSAS

Springfield

Marionville

Branson

Burfordville

Whitewater River

OKLAHOMA

ARKANSAS

TENNESSEE

KENTUCKY

STATE SYMBOLS

State American folk dance: Square dance

State animal: Missouri mule

State aquatic animal: Paddlefish

State bird: Eastern Bluebird

State fish: Channel catfish

State flower: White hawthorn blossom

State fossil: Crinoid

State insect: Honeybee

State mineral: Galena

State musical instrument: Fiddle

State rock: Mozarkite

State tree: Flowering dogwood

State tree nut: Black walnut

State seal

That was a great trip! We have traveled all over Missouri! There are a few places that we didn't have time for, though. Next time, we plan to visit Hallmark Visitors' Center in Kansas City. We'll learn how greeting cards are made. If we're lucky, we'll even get to watch some artists and technicians!

STATE SONG

"MISSOURI WALTZ"

Words by James R. Shannon, music by John V. Eppel

Hush-a-bye, ma baby,
  slumbertime is comin' soon;
Rest yo' head upon my breast
  while Mommy hums a tune;
The sandman is callin' where
  shadows are fallin',
While the soft breezes sigh as in
  days long gone by.
Way down in Missouri where I
  heard this melody,
When I was a little child upon my
  Mommy's knee;
The old folks were hummin'; their
  banjos were strummin';
So sweet and low.
Strum, strum, strum, strum, strum,
Seems I hear those banjos playin'
  once again,
Hum, hum, hum, hum, hum,
That same old plaintive strain.
Hear that mournful melody,

It just haunts you the whole day
  long,
And you wander in dreams back
  to Dixie, it seems,
When you hear that old time
  song.
Hush-a-bye ma baby, go to sleep
  on Mommy's knee,
Journey back to Dixieland in
  dreams again with me;
It seems like your Mommy is there
  once again,
And the old folks were strummin'
  that same old refrain.
Way down in Missouri where I
  learned this lullaby,
When the stars were blinkin' and
  the moon was climbin' high,
Seems I hear voices low, as in
  days long ago,
Singin' hush-a-bye.

State flag

FAMOUS PEOPLE

Angelou, Maya (1928–2014), poet and civil rights activist

Bacharach, Burt (1928–), composer

Baker, Josephine (1906–1975), entertainer

Berra, Yogi (1925–2015), baseball player

Carver, George Washington (1864–1943), educator, botanist

Cheadle, Don (1964–), actor

Copeland, Misty (1982–), ballet dancer

Cronkite, Walter (1916–2009), television broadcast journalist

Eliot, T. S. (1888–1965), poet

Hamm, Jon (1971–), actor

Hubble, Edwin (1889–1953), astronomer

Hughes, Langston (1902–1967), author and poet

James, Jesse (1847–1882), outlaw

Kemper, Ellie (1980–), actress

Lester, Julius (1939–), children's author

Pulitzer, Joseph (1847–1911), journalist and publisher

Ross, Nellie Tayloe (1876–1977), first woman governor of a state

Truman, Harry S. (1884–1972), 33rd U.S. president

Twain, Mark (pen name of Samuel Clemens) (1835–1910), author

Van Dyke, Dick (1925–), comedic actor

Wilder, Laura Ingalls (1867–1957), children's author

Wilkins, Roy (1901–1981), civil rights leader

WORDS TO KNOW

albinos (al-BYE-nohz) animals with white hair, light skin, and pink eyes

arch (ARCH) something curved like an upside-down letter *U*

cannonball (KAN-uhn-bawl) a big ball that's shot out of a cannon

compromise (KOM-pruh-mize) an agreement in which both sides get something and give up something

culture (KUHL-chur) a group of people's beliefs, customs, and ways of life

heritage (HAYR-uh-tij) customs and ways of life passed down over time

industry (IN-duh-stree) a type of business

missionaries (MISH-uh-nayr-eez) people who try to spread their religion in an area

obedience (oh-BEE-dee-uhnss) the act of obeying directions

pioneer (pye-uh-NEER) a person who moves into an unsettled land

traditions (truh-DISH-uhnz) long-held customs and ways of doing things

tributary (TRIB-yuh-tayr-ee) a river that flows into a bigger river

TO LEARN MORE

IN THE LIBRARY

Kerley, Barbara. *The Extraordinary Mark Twain (According to Susy)*. New York, NY: Scholastic Press, 2010.

Koontz, Robin. *What's Great About Missouri?* Minneapolis, MN: Lerner Publications, 2015.

Strait, James. *Weird Missouri: Your Travel Guide to Missouri's Local Legends and Best Kept Secrets*. New York, NY: Sterling Publishing, 2008.

ON THE WEB

Visit our Web site for links about Missouri:

childsworld.com/links

Note to Parents, Teachers, and Librarians: We routinely verify our Web links to make sure they are safe and active sites. So encourage your readers to check them out!

PLACES TO VISIT OR CONTACT

Missouri Welcome Center

visitmo.com

1700 Route 61 South

Hannibal, MO 63401

573/248-2420

For more information about traveling in Missouri

The State Historical Society of Missouri

shsmo.org

One University Blvd.

Saint Louis, MO 63121

314/516-5143

For more information about the history of Missouri

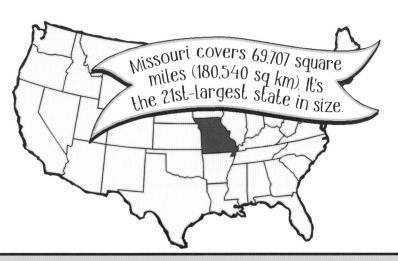

Missouri covers 69,707 square miles (180,540 sq km). It's the 21st-largest state in size.

INDEX

A

Adventures of Tom Sawyer, The, (Mark Twain), 35
African Americans, 22, 23
Air and Space Exhibit, 31
American Plunge, 11
Athens, 23

B

Bagnell Dam, 9
Battle of Athens State Historic Site, 23
Benton, Thomas Hart, 29
Boeing Company, 30-31
Bollinger Mill, 24-25
Branson, 10
Burfordville, 25
Burfordville Covered Bridge, 25
Burgers' Smokehouse, 33

C

Cape County Milling Company, 25
Carver, George Washington, 9
caves, 4, 7
Clark, William, 16
Clemens, Samuel Langhorne, 34

D

Diamond, 9
Dred Scott case, 22

F

farming, 7, 16, 27, 31
French explorers, 15
Frisco Steam Train, 11
fur traders, 14-15

G

Gateway Arch, 18-19
General Assembly, 28

Germans, 20-21
governors, 22

H

Hannibal, 34-35
Harry S. Truman Reservoir, 6
Hermann, 20-21

I

ice cream cones, 30
Independence, 16-17, 29
International Bowling Museum, 18

J

James S. McDonnell Prologue Room, 31
Jefferson City, 28-29
Joliet, Louis, 14
judges, 28

K

Kansas City, 9, 21, 24, 33
Kirksville, 26

L

Lake of the Ozarks, 6, 8-9
Lee's Summit, 16
Lewis, Meriwether, 16
Liguest, Pierre Laclède, 14

M

Maifest, 20
Marionville, 12-13
Mark Twain Cave, 34
Marmaros, 10
Marquette, Jacques, 14
Marshall, 27
Marvel Cave, 10
McDonnell, James, 30
McDonnell Douglas Corporation, 30-31

Meramec Caverns, 6-7
missionaries, 15
Mississippi River, 7, 14, 15
Missouri Compromise, 22
Missouri River, 7, 14
Missouri State Corn Husking Championship, 27
Missouri Town 1855, 16

N

National Frontier Trails Center, 17
national parks, 13
Native Americans, 15
Neosho, 29

O

Octoberfest, 20
Old Tyme Apple Festival, 26
Oregon Trail, 16
Osage River, 9
Ozark Cavefish National Wildlife Refuge, 13
Ozark Mountains, 7

P

pioneers, 11, 16, 17, 19
Pony Express National Museum, 17
population, 21
Purina Farms, 32

S

Saint Joseph, 17
Saint Louis, 9, 14, 16, 18-19, 21, 22, 24, 30, 31
Saint Louis Science Center, 19
Saline County Fair, 27
Santa Fe Trail, 16
Scott, Dred, 22
settlers, 16, 20
Silver Dollar City, 10-11
slavery, 23

soybeans, 24, 26, 27
spacecraft, 31
sports, 8-9
Springfield, 13, 21, 22
Stage Curtain, 6
state bird, 13
state capital, 29
state capitol, 28
state flower, 13
state motto, 29
state nickname, 5
state tree, 13
statehood, 17
Ste. Geneviève, 15, 21

T

Tom Sawyer Days, 35
Truman, Harry S., 4, 29
Twain, Mark, 4, 34-35

U

U.S. Civil War, 22-23

V

Versailles, 26

W

white squirrels, 4, 12-13
Whitewater River, 25
Wilson's Creek National Battlefield, 22
World War II, 29
Wurstfest, 20

Bye, Show-Me State. We had a great time. We'll come back soon!